Shamanism Explained

Shamanism Guide for Beginners

Shamanism Overview, Shamanic Principles, Healing and Rituals, Cycle of Life, Time Manipulation, Shamanic Maps beyond Death and More!

By Riley Star

Copyrights and Trademarks

All rights reserved. No part of this book may be reproduced or transformed in any form or by any means, graphic, electronic, or mechanical, including photocopying, recording, taping, or by any information storage retrieval system, without the written permission of the author.

This publication is Copyright ©2018 NRB Publishing, an imprint. Nevada. All products, graphics, publications, software and services mentioned and recommended in this publication are protected by trademarks. In such instance, all trademarks & copyright belong to the respective owners. For information consult www.NRBpublishing.com

Disclaimer and Legal Notice

This product is not legal, medical, or accounting advice and should not be interpreted in that manner. You need to do your own due-diligence to determine if the content of this product is right for you. While every attempt has been made to verify the information shared in this publication, neither the author, neither publisher, nor the affiliates assume any responsibility for errors, omissions or contrary interpretation of the subject matter herein. Any perceived slights to any specific person(s) or organization(s) are purely unintentional.

We have no control over the nature, content and availability of the web sites listed in this book. The inclusion of any web site links does not necessarily imply a recommendation or endorse the views expressed within them. We take no responsibility for, and will not be liable for, the websites being temporarily unavailable or being removed from the internet.

The accuracy and completeness of information provided herein and opinions stated herein are not guaranteed or warranted to produce any particular results, and the advice and strategies, contained herein may not be suitable for every individual. Neither the author nor the publisher shall be liable for any loss incurred as a consequence of the use and application, directly or indirectly, of any information presented in this work. This publication is designed to provide information in regard to the subject matter covered.

Neither the author nor the publisher assume any responsibility for any errors or omissions, nor do they represent or warrant that the ideas, information, actions, plans, suggestions contained in this book is in all cases accurate. It is the reader's responsibility to find advice before putting anything written in this book into practice. The information in this book is not intended to serve as legal, medical, or accounting advice.

Foreword

Shamans are one of the oldest and most enduring ancient figures in history. During the ancient times, shamanism is part of some people's religions and magic rituals as it is an archaic method that can be traced back around the Paleolithic era. The elements and principles of Shamanism in other countries and cultures are essentially similar to one another despite of the different time periods. There are only some surface details differences in the principles, and also the way a culture or country applies these principles and techniques.

The elemental requirements, underlying fundamentals, and human psyche are the foundations of this ancient art that has remained constant throughout the ages. It is quite remarkable that this practice has survived over thousands of years, and has been incorporated in many other religious and magical systems in the world. Shamans are known as the world's healers; however, as societies evolve and progressed, the roles of the shamans are being fulfilled by others. Shamanism has become one of the systems that brought about other artistic endeavors like theater, dancing, religious rituals, ceremonial magic, music as well as writing and language. It can be traced back from different customs and traditions, folklores and myth as well as other beliefs. It is usually used to manipulate the universe's hidden forces in making one's life better.

Today, many western nationals are turning to this ancient art as a way to revitalize and integrate themselves into an outlook that's beyond what is being offered in their own cultures. Recently, many people despite of the advances of today's modern technology are increasingly becoming interested in the world of Shamans. Fortunately, with the advent of the internet, many people can now learn the secrets and methods of this ancient system that was once just limited to people taking up anthropology or ethnology. There are now online courses available as well as seminars and workshops that also include things like fire walking. Some people are now devouring the ancient wisdom from different tribes through books about shamanism as it is now more accessible.

This book will cover the basic things that a beginner needs to know about Shamanism. We have included the principles and methods used by Shamans but we made it in a way where anyone can do it and apply it in their daily lives. You don't need to know all the nuts and bolts of everything about Shamanism, but it's important that you understand the underlying principles of this system and master the ways of how you can apply it and integrate it in your own life.

Table of Contents

Introduction to Shamanism and Brief History 1

    Origins of Shamanism 4

Chapter One: Understanding Shamanism 7

    How Can You Become a Shaman 9

    Qualities of Shamans 11

    Benefits of Shamanism 14

Chapter Two: The Basics of Shamanism: Imagination and Visualization 19

    The Power of Imagination According to Shamans 20

    How People Limit One's Imagination 22

    Why Do You Need to Use Imagination? 26

    Visualization Exercises 28

Chapter Three: The Basics of Shamanism: Web Power and Human Spirit Body 35

    Web Power 36

    The Human Spirit Body 38

Chapter Four: Spirit Helpers 43

    Power of Rocks 45

    Power of Animals 47

    Power of Plants 50

Chapter Five: Shaping Time and Learning to be in the Present 53

- Shaping Time 54
  - Stretching Time 55
  - Contracting Time 57
  - Flying to the Future 58
- Developing Presence 59
- Chapter Six: The Circle of Life 63
  - Creation and Destruction 64
    - Letting Go of Possessions 66
    - Letting Go of Beliefs 67
    - Letting Go of Habits 71
    - Letting Go of Relationships 72
  - Creation 75
- Chapter Seven: The Worlds of Shamanic Journey 79
  - The Lower World 80
  - The Upper World 81
  - The Middle World 83
- Chapter Eight: Shamanic Healing 85
  - Hollow Bone Concept 86
  - Soul Retrieval 88
  - Reliving the Moment 89
- Chapter Nine: Ritual and Ceremonies of Shamanism 91
  - Rituals and Ceremonies 92

Characteristic of Rituals and Ceremonies 93
Symbolic Death Rites 97
Shamanic Maps to the Journey beyond Death 101
Chapter Ten: Bringing Shamanism to Life 103
How to Bring Shamanism to Life 104
Morning Messenger 105
Inviting Your Power Animals.. 106
Photo Credits... 109
References 111

Introduction to Shamanism and Brief History

Imagination in Shamanism is more than just a brain activity; rather it is the main vehicle that carries a shaman to unknown realms. According to Shamanistic principles, thoughts and feelings are forms of energy that can go to different "worlds," and it's not just some kind of mental exercise that most of us are taught to believe.

Introduction to Shamanism and Brief History

During the ancient times and throughout the history, Shamans fulfill different roles like poets, artists, healers, mediators, and the one who facilitates ceremonies. They are also known as someone who can predict the future and prophesy one. They also help people if they need access to lost knowledge, and teach them on how to develop mental abilities. There are a lot of shamans who are healers, they've master and learned the art of using herbal plants as medicines, and they also know how to perform healing rituals to aid the sick. Other shamans know how to predict the weather, locate good opportunities, and even suspend the laws of physics and the laws of space and time. Shamans can be found in Asia, Africa, North America, South America, and even in Europe. During the ancient times, healer shamans are usually located in Tibet, India and also Siberia. There are also lots of Shamans in Japan. They all share the same psychic abilities and have master the art of imagination.

"Shaman" came from a Siberian word called "Saman, which originally referred to male practitioners. "Shamanka" refers to female shamans. According to the principles of

Introduction to Shamanism and Brief History

Shamanism, the universe is composed of different dimensions containing a celestial world and chtonic underworld that are filled with various spirit rulers and other spiritual beings. Each level of the universe is connected with a central axis that resembles a world tree. It is through this central axis that lets shamans gain access to different dimensions of the universe.

Another important fundamental in Shamanism is that animals and humans as well as other things in life are all equal. They believe that all of us are one with nature. This principle of equality is expressed during rituals wherein it appeases the souls of the dead creatures. They arrange the skulls of the dead animals in a certain direction where the place of rebirth is found. American Indians and Finnish natives integrate this principle when performing rites. Another related concept is called Metamorphosis. This is where humans and animals have the ability to assume each other's shape. In South America and Asian culture, this is known as "Doppelganger" where people, animals, and spiritual beings are interchangeable. The gateway between worlds, according to Shamanistic principles is the entrance to where ancestral spirits as well as demons dwell. It can be represented by icebergs, clashing rocks, and a monster's jaws during rituals.

Origins of Shamanism

No one knows exactly where the concept of Shamanism came from but according to ancient historians, many researchers and anthropologists from all over the world agree that the fundamentals of this system began when the first Paleo – Americans moved across the Bering land bridge that connected Siberia and Alaska some 12,000 years ago.

According to R.G. Wasson, he's an ethnobiologist, and he said that Shamanism may have come from many cultures where psychotropic plants are associated. In Shamanism, there are around eighty various types of these psychotropic plants used during rituals and healing ceremonies particularly in South America. These plants are also accompanied with drumming, singing, dancing, and

Introduction to Shamanism and Brief History

endurance tests like fire walking during rituals or ceremonies.

Shamanism is still relevant today as it was during the ancient times but it highly depends on how a person approaches it. In an era where information is transmitted easily and conveniently, the real value of this ancient system lies in recovering the knowledge from oneself, and also how one can relate to other people. Shamanism can teach the modern world about how we as a culture and as an individual can regain the spirit of our collective past, and form a connection with these shamans, and those people that lived before us. Shamanism can be a ways to reconnect oneself with other people and the world around us despite of cultural differences and beliefs.

Chapter One: Understanding Shamanism

Shamans are known as the mediator of humans and its relation to the celestial world including spirits and omens. Society has endured the hunter – gatherer stage for many years, and as we began moving to the agricultural stage and towards a more developed way of living, the shamans took in religious roles because they began developing priesthood. According to Alvin Toffler, the societies today are suffering from future shock, which is why some people are trying to integrate shamanistic principles in their day to day lives. In the west, traditions and cultural

Chapter One: Understanding Shamanism

gaps are now accepting Shamanism. If someone is really trying to learn and practice the underlying principles that Shamanism imparts then people can possibly have the ability to freely enter the different dimensions of the universe and access certain powers that one can use to improve one's inner self. This is because the deeper sections of the mind can now speak to you in terms of different symbols. There are lots of belief systems, Shamanism included, wherein we can use certain principles in varying degrees to achieve success. One of which is imagination. This is very important when it comes to studying Shamanism. The idea of spiritual progress is synonymous because we have a belief that if we change ourselves, therefore we can change our society, and it all starts with the mind.

This chapter will provide you with the basic principles of Shamanism, how a person can become a Shaman, and the benefits of learning from this ancient belief system.

Chapter One: Understanding Shamanism

How Can You Become a Shaman

There are 3 ways that people are initiated into the art of Shamanism, these are the following:

- Self – Selected: It's your own choice to study this system for some reason.
- Selection by Older Shamans: You are selected to be trained by older shamans especially if you have survived some sort of catastrophe or life – threatening incidents
- Inherited: If you've inherited the role from your parents.

There are also other cases on how people got interested into this belief system; maybe you're a student and have become interested in this art, or your friend and other family members have taught you some things, or you just deliberately like the idea of becoming a Shaman for personal purposes, whatever your selection method is, shamans have traditionally underwent training for a long time. Usually, before you become a shaman in your own right, you need to be able to pass certain rigorous test or at least satisfy your master/ mentor. However, it doesn't mean that you can't become a shaman if you don't go through these trainings or brutal initiation since there are now lots of ordinary people who have learned the different techniques and have successfully applied it in their own lives. You can use the techniques you'll learn here to create a more enriching life.

Keep in mind that Shamanism, just like other religious or belief systems, will not eliminate all your problems in life – that's impossible because problems are part of life. Instead, Shamanistic principles can teach a person on how they can better deal and solve any problems they'll encounter along the way, and perhaps respond to it in a more optimistic approach. You still have to take action in order to get the results that you want, and along with Shamanistic techniques, you can be more successful in attaining those results.

You can use your Shamanic abilities by being able to position yourself in the right place at the right time. And once you've done that, the rest is up to you. You need to now depend on your innate abilities to overcome any obstacles that life presents but given the edge that you have, you'll have a much easier time in dealing with life in general.

Qualities of Shamans

What makes shamans different from other people in their communities? What do shamans possess that makes them powerful? What do they know that gives them the ability to heal or cope with life better? There are many qualities and mindset that make a shaman. If you are serious at becoming one, then you might want to really read this section because it will give you a sneak peek as to the kind of characteristic that the shamans possess.

- Shamans know that life and the universe is made up of energy. They know how the environment or nature relates to the human body. They know how to recognize the innate power in themselves and in nature, and how everything is connected. They also know that we are spiritual beings, and shamans know how to tap into it.

Chapter One: Understanding Shamanism

- The shamans know how to stay relaxed including their physical bodies because in this way, they can reduce their stress levels to become more efficient. They have the ability to quiet down any form of negative thoughts so that they can have a better perspective or perhaps hear their mind and heart's internal message.

- Shamans know how to use their imagination. They have learned the ability to recognize symbols and clues that will help them in gathering knowledge. They also trust their inner compass.

- They are artists by nature because they know how to use images and symbols and interpret it as a way to overcome problems. These symbolisms are often expressed in dance rituals, songs, and other movements.

- Shamans have an excellent insight into other's characters. They understand people, and have learned to detach themselves from any dramas of life. They also find ways on how to amuse themselves and laugh at the human condition or circumstances; in short they don't take themselves or life 'seriously.'

- They know how communicate internally and externally. They know how to alter their views and also suspend any limitations of the mind especially when it comes to beliefs.

- Shamans know how to be successful in life and they also know when to take action. They are practical and also comfortable with the paradox of life.

- They are flexible individuals who know how to shift their levels of consciousness at will.

- Shamans are fighters, and they're also persistent, and disciplined individuals. They also know how to protect themselves from unforeseen circumstances.

Chapter One: Understanding Shamanism

The qualities mentioned above are all shared by shamans from different cultures over the years. They are ordinary people like you and me who have developed themselves out of pure dedication and passion. Their talents are no greater than everyone's capability to become successful or achieve similar levels but perhaps the difference is that they know how to tap into their innate abilities and the universe' powers and use it to their advantage. The techniques and methods of Shamanism can work well even in today's modern life because the art of Shamanism is a strategy for gaining power which you can apply in your day to day life but it will work best if you'll learn the mindset, characteristics, and attitudes of Shamans.

Benefits of Shamanism

Here are the benefits you can get from learning about Shamanism or practicing this ancient art.

- Your ideas about life's circumstances and how they affect you and those around you will make you have a better perspective in life. It will allow you to have

Chapter One: Understanding Shamanism

more freedom because your concepts about linear time will be changed.

- You will understand that you can take charge of your life, and that there's something higher than you that can transform you. You won't feel as though, you're the victim of circumstances.

- You'll begin to contemplate and appreciate how you are related to life in general, and you'll have a much broader perspective.

- You'll understand reality's nature, and your dreams will undergo through some form of radical transformation because you'll then discover how you can set appropriate goals for yourself and bring them to completion.

- Your understanding of what real power is will change and be more enhanced. In some ways, it will make you humble as well.

- Your method of communication and relation to other people will improve. You'll also gain a new perspective into the real meaning of compassion because you'll understand yourself more and also others better.

- You'll feel challenged by the problems that will come your way, but you'll also feel inspired because of it. You'll know how to handle adversity better, and avoid or let go of the things you cannot control.

- You'll learn how to gain knowledge and information through your inner guidance.

- You'll learn how to become more relax and stay graceful even under pressure especially whenever you're facing adversities.

Before you can develop your shamanic abilities, the first thing you need to do is learn the basic of life – energy. You need to understand how it works, not on a scientific level but more on a spiritual level. Your thoughts and emotions

Chapter One: Understanding Shamanism

direct the energy in your physical being and also those around you. It can bring about the results you want both in the real world and the spiritual world. It will help you create the life you always wanted. You'll also understand the human spirit, and manage the energy within your body in a way that will energize you rather than depletes you. Once you study shamanism, you'll learn how to ground and protect yourself, and you'll also discover how you can develop your own innate power in creating personal gateways through mastery.

Shamanism is all about learning the systems of knowledge that predates your social, cultural, and familial conditioning It will force you to unlearn things, and guide you in how you can apprehend the world despite of the confusion dogmas, theologies, and beliefs that exists. Mastering the art of shamanism will make you become the universe's co – creator, you'll become a catalyst in human evolution, help you release yourself from isolation, and leads you to align yourself with nature's healing powers. You'll find balance in your life and most importantly, you'll know who you are and where you want to go. Shamanism can help you discover your true purpose.

Chapter One: Understanding Shamanism

Chapter Two: The Basics of Shamanism: Imagination and Visualization

As part of the modern society, most of the people today don't quite know how imagination works. Our power to use our imagination sometime seems so illogical and even irrational yet this is one of the greatest innate abilities that allow us to realize our dreams and create the kind of world we want to live in. If you think about it, incredible feats in human history and everything you see in reality all began with an idea, and was molded through imagination. Most of the time, we use to be sort of skeptical about it because it gives us a sense of false illusions but we admire its astounding effects. People are usually uncomfortable with the fear of not being able to control our imagination yet we all tend to be amazed by the visions and hope that it brings. We even doubt its usefulness in the face of logic but we take pleasure in the images we see because of it. Sometimes people tend to think that imagination stops the moment we leave childhood but in reality, this ability can be a source of pure creativity if we just know how to develop it and use it.

This chapter is all about how shamans tap into their imagination and harness its incredible power through visualization. As mentioned earlier, imagination is one of the fundamentals of Shamanism, without it one can never enter the different realms of the universe.

The Power of Imagination According to Shamans

From shamanistic point of view, imagination is more than just a brain activity. To them, imagination is one of the most vital vehicles of humans that will link us to the web of power and to the spiritual/ celestial world. Imagination is the first step if you want to learn the art of Shamanism because this is how an individual can gain access to the world of "non – ordinary reality," as Michael Harner puts it.

Children that are born with this innate ability tend to forget about it as they grow up because of enculturation. They were taught that there's always a logical explanation to whatever's happening in the physical world, and there's nothing wrong with that, it's just that the power of imagination tends to diminish away as each of us attempt to master the cultural ways and physical things around us so that we can adapt to "reality." Therefore the door that connects us to the spiritual world or the higher universe as some people calls it begins to close in our minds, though to a degree, this is also essential if you want to be able to identify the difference between the physical world and the spiritual realm. The only difference with shamans is that they don't lose track of this innate ability and they apply it in their daily lives just as how they master the logic of the physical world. They tend to focus but don't get fully lost in memory.

Chapter Two: The Basics of Shamanism: C

Learning shamanic skills means that you need to reopen your door of imagination if you truly want to strengthen the link between the physical and non – physical. You need to re – establish this pathway through visualization techniques and various shamanic visioning methods which we will delve on later. These techniques are very convenient and quite simple but perhaps not easy to do especially if you haven't been using your imagination lately. Don't worry though, because you don't need to achieve the highest level of mental abilities to do this especially if your mind tends to become a bit rusty or you probably have a hard time focusing, but practicing such techniques more often can definitely help you in being in control of this innate power.

How People Limit One's Imagination

I'm sure you have heard the saying that "Imagination's the limit" all the time, but in reality it's not your imagination that is limited, rather it is your belief that your imagination has a limit. Today, many modern – day philosophers, physicists, and metaphysical practitioners agree that being able to imagine is very important because it is one of the main things that brings people to success. In fact, most of them now suggest that people should change the quote of "I'll believe it once I see it" to "I'll see it when I believe it." This means that you must first see things in your mind, and feel it as if it's already there, as if it's reality because that will bring forth its fruition. If you can see it in your mind, one day you can see it for real.

This is where Shamans are experts at. They are very aware of this perspective and they know how to create it for themselves. Shamans know the importance of being able to see the result before it actualizes physically. They are also aware that people can only achieve certain things as much as they can truly imagine for themselves, that's why they tend to work at themselves first by enhancing their personal abilities to have, do or be. In short, one's ability to imagine raises an individual's ability to have things in life. And just like a muscle, imagination needs to be stretched, used, exercised, and strengthen. Shamanism will teach you using various strategies on how you can use this tool to expand your imagination, and lose any kind of limiting beliefs.

Chapter Two: The Basics of Shamanism: C

A great example when it comes to limiting beliefs and power of imagination is when people suddenly gained a huge sum of money either from inheritance or winning the lottery; studies have shown that most of the time, the people who gained this huge amount were unable to hold on to it due to mismanagement or they simply just squander it, and made poor investment decisions. This is because they, mentally speaking, are not prepared to handle such huge amount, and that's mainly because of their personal limiting beliefs.

You see, even if your physical situation has changed, you won't be able to sustain it or make the most out of it, IF your beliefs don't change. This is because the physical body has a certain comfort level known as the homeostasis state. In financial terms, this is known as "financial thermostat." You can have a million dollars but if your mind is set only for thousands, you'll tend to spend it away without you even knowing it because your mind will need to get back to its "normal financial level." You have set limiting beliefs that you only deserve to earn this much or that much, and anything that goes beyond that is quite frightening for the physical body. Just like animals, humans need to be persuaded to form new perspectives about certain things. To the physical body, any kind of change is very scary because it's representing the unfamiliar or the unknown. This is the reason why "fear of success" happens to some people; even if on the surface they dreamt of becoming successful, and has done everything to achieve it, once they have it they'll tend to sabotage their own selves because their minds are not mentally prepared to handle the fortune or success mainly due to limiting beliefs and poor imagination. They want it but if you dig deeper the unconsciously are afraid of it for some reason, most of the time it's because they think they don't deserve to be one.

The Shamans knows this, and they have worked their way to adjust their "success levels" by using their power of imagination and transforming any negative or limiting beliefs about things. One can even say that they hacked their own brain or tricked their own mind to let go such beliefs that limits them from becoming who they truly want to be.

Chapter Two: The Basics of Shamanism: C

Why Do You Need to Use Imagination?

Shamans use the power of imagination if they want to retrieve certain information or ask for some spiritual guidance. They imagine what they want to look for, and to them this is the first thing that one needs to do to achieve any result. Imagining what you want is necessary if say, you need to find a parking place, or earn financial figures. Whether you know it or not, you subconsciously use your imagination whenever you're being confronted with a new challenge. You use it to choose what question you need to ask, you use it to help you decide where you should focus on. Imagination helps humans create a vivid picture that will help in seeing or feeling whatever it is we're trying to get, and then we act on those picture we see in our minds.

Visualization is a technique that's commonly used to enhance one's imagination. It is where you can create mental picture of the exact things or circumstances that you want to happen. A very simple example is that if you want to own a new car, you can create an image of you riding it and seeing it as vividly and as detailed as you can, and feeling the same feeling when you already have it. You can concentrate on this over and over until you get results, though action may be needed but imagination can motivate you to do what needs to be done. It's a very effect technique that shamans used for centuries to help them manifest the end result that they want to achieve. They learned how to manipulate their own thoughts and feelings to create a sense – oriented picture of their dreams. Here's how they do visualization:

- First and foremost, you need to create a mental picture of the exact thing or experience that you want to have in reality. Say, a new house or car, you and your loved one on a trip or vacation, you getting promoted or receiving an award.

- Make sure to describe the end result it in great detail. Not the process of how you'll get it but the outcome. Try to see it as clearly as you can as if it's already there.

- Include all your emotions and senses whenever you're creating the image in your mind. Add reactions such as excitement or gratefulness. Feel the feelings of how you'll respond once you see it or experience. Infuse all of this as you create the mental picture in your head.

- Let it go, and repeat the exercise at least 10 times a day or more often.

Visualization Exercises

According to shamanism, the key to a successful visualization is to add another dimension to it through integrating nature and using all of the senses. The spirit of all of nature to them is the true source of power. Natural beings and nature itself is 3 – dimensional which is why shamans re – create their visions in a 3 – dimensional way by incorporation the senses of sound, sight, smell, touch, and even taste.

As an example, say you're to re – create or imagine an apple, what you need to do to "see it" in your mind is to imagine feeling the apple in your hands, imagine how it smells, and hear the crunch as you bite and taste it.

Chapter Two: The Basics of Shamanism: C

Another important thing to keep in mind is to use your natural surroundings to further enhance your visualization. Say for example, you're imaging yourself relaxing on a beach in a soft surface; you may want to sit on or lie down on something that's really soft or cushiony because it will aid your ability to really picture whatever's in your mind. According to shamans, natural objects like grass, climate or soil have more power than synthetic materials so try to incorporate it when you're doing visualization. Here are some exercises you can try to increase your focus and your senses:

Exercise #1:

Step #1: Close your eyes and make sure to relax your body.

Step #2: Using your sense of touch, you can explore your surrounding

Step #3: Try to listen to all the sounds around you

Step #4: Make sure to notice all the smells around you and the overall atmosphere

Step #5: Notice all of the 3 senses simultaneously.

Exercise #2:

Step #1: Choose a certain fruit and see it physically

Step #2: Close your eyes, and picture the fruit in your mind. Feel it in your hands

Step #3: Smell the fruit and begin to eat it

Step #4: Focus on the taste of the apple

Exercise #3:

Step #1: Choose a physical object

Step #2: Close your eyes and relax

Step #3: Re – create that object in your mind

Step #4: Focus on the aspects of the object and see it in great detail using all your senses

Step #5: Describe each of the object's quality in natural terms or as vivid as you can

Step #6: Imagine the picture changes using natural qualities

Chapter Two: The Basics of Shamanism: C

Relaxation Technique

Learning to relax the body and the mind is one of the things that shamans are experts at. It's very helpful especially when you're trying to re – create scenarios or experiences you want to have like journeying with a spirit guide. If you cultivate the art of relaxation, you'll get lots of benefits physically, emotionally, and mentally. The more you relax your body, the more powerful your experience will be. There are many ways on how you can relax your body but the steps we listed below is highly recommended because it has proved effective for many people but of course you can try other methods of relaxation that works best for you. Practicing it as often as you can will make you reach deep levels of relaxation rapidly.

Exercise #1:

Step #1: Find a safe and comfy place where you wouldn't be interrupted. It's also best if your turn the lights down low, and lie on your back with your body fully stretched out

Step #2: Before you begin, it's best that you take 3 deep breaths from your diaphragm to release any sort of tension that you're currently feeling.

Step #3: Start to become aware of your body. Feel your feet, and gradually move upward in each of your body parts until you reach your head.

Step #4: Notice the gravity's effect on your body as it pulls you downward making your body parts and internal organs pressed against the floor or carpet you're lying in. Feel the inertia on your face, and realize how gravity gives your body a weight that will keep you from floating up and drifting.

Step #5: Let go of any resistance. It's a natural force on earth so just give in to it. Allow it to pull you back along with all your tensions and inhibitions. Let this natural force go back into the earth.

Step #6: At the same time be aware that your thoughts and mental images are not subject to any natural force like gravity. Realize that with your mind, you can go wherever you want to go without anything pulling you back.

Chapter Three: The Basics of Shamanism: Web Power and Human Spirit Body

Web Power is one of the basic principles in Shamanism. To the shamans, this concept or notion that all physical things have "spirit" within them, this is something that underlies all of life. In the world of shamans, web power is the force that gives meaning to everything and makes everything coherent, and without this the world would be chaotic. To the shamans, the web power is not a theory but a definite reality that's the same as the force of gravity or other

Chapter Three: Web Power and Human Spirit Body

laws of the universe. For the shamans, web power is one of the keys to success.

This chapter will delve into the next basic principles of Shamanism which is web power and the spirit realm. You'll also learn another set of exercises that you can do to enhance this ability and better understand this concept.

Web Power

To the Shamans, the spirit realm is very important in their world view. Understanding the physical realm through modern day science is essential but not adequate if the spiritual realm is not in the picture. Without the knowledge and mastery of web power, Shamans believe that a person is truly a victim of circumstance because one cannot learn how to control their own actions.

According to Shamanistic principles, the world of spirit is within all of us in all forms but of course it is hidden unless an individual learns how to see through it. This is why it's important to learn about this principle and familiarize yourself with it if you wanted to become a Shaman because it will enable you to open your senses and

Chapter Three: Web Power and Human Spirit Body

unveil the knowledge and power contained within this realm.

According to the Shamans, everything is made up of the same material. Humans, animals, trees, water, rocks, wind etc. in its core are all made up of the same material. If you take a rock for example and break it down to its atomic and subatomic level, you'll find that there's only a space or spirit. From the shamanic point of view, the spirit is within everything and every other form of life both the inanimate and the animated objects. To them, the source of energy which is the spirit is what you'll use to communicate with mentally. It is this communication with a thing's spirit is what empowers shamans because they know the invisible web of power which is the spirit is the real source of life, even in inanimate objects. To the shamans, if a person knows how to communicate with the spirit of things, one can gain a much deeper understanding of how the universe works. When you learned how to properly use the web of power, you'll also learn how to channel it appropriately.

Chapter Three: Web Power and Human Spirit Body

As a concrete example, you might know of some people who communicate with plants while they're watering it in order for the plant to properly grow, and make the spirit of the plant feel like it is truly being valued and taken care of.

The Human Spirit Body

When it comes to the human spirit body, according to the shamans, it is unique and different. The spirit within each of us is linked with heat. For the shamans, the spirit body interpenetrates the physical body and it is made up of a various vibrant colors.

The spirit body is a sort of fluid energy that extends outside the physical body giving it like a glow or what others call a certain aura. The spirit body responds to the thought, reactions, and feelings of an individual to any circumstances through expansion, contraction or a change in the color/ aura. Therefore, the human spirit body can instantly tell how an individual is feeling at any given

Chapter Three: Web Power and Human Spirit Body

moment. It's an energetic field that one projects depending on what they're thinking and feeling.

If a person has learned on how to get rid of negative emotions or energy with its own positive vibes then that person can work or be at any type of negative situation without being affected or influenced by these negativities. An individual with positive thoughts and emotions sort of carry a high level of this positivity making low level negativity useless since it can't penetrate one's positive mind and spirit.

This goes to say that, one of the keys to success is being aware of the changes and states of your human spirit body. It is through awareness and knowledge that can give a person full control to oneself despite of how other people perceives you. If you learn how to be sensitive to your own energetic fluctuations, you can gain power over any situation. The best way to understand the human spirit body is through observing oneself. Observation is how you can self – record your spirit or body's reaction to certain things.

Chapter Three: Web Power and Human Spirit Body

For example, if someone screams at you, your instant or default reaction to that is to feel being verbally attacked, insulted, or disrespected. Such emotional feelings can remain with you for a very long time even after that incident. Usually, the negative reactions of the human spirit body manifests later on in some physical way. You can also use the human spirit body when trying to decipher how other people feel at the moment, say if there's some form of tension or stress, your spirit body can detect that if you just know how to pay attention to it since it responds directly to thoughts and feelings. Here are some exercises you can try to become aware of your human spirit body and tap into your web power:

Exercise #1: Feeling Your Spirit Self

Step #1: Relax and close your eyes

Step #2: Try to discover the edges/ aura of your body

Step #3: Expand these edges to about a few inches

Step #4: Experiment with how you can further expand this energy field or aura

Step #5: Shrink it back to its original size

Chapter Three: Web Power and Human Spirit Body

Exercise #2: Seeing Your Spirit Self

Step #1: Relax your body and close your eyes

Step #2: Visualize that there's a field of energy around your body

Step #3: Try to notice and observe the quality and colors of the energy

Step #4: After doing the exercise, you can pose a question to what you've observed, although this is optional.

Exercise #3: Reassessing Your Spirit Self

Step #1: Relax and close your eyes

Step #2: Get a sense of your human spirit body

Step #3: Scan this spirit body and notice it

Step #4: Direct the energy to the missing areas

Step #5: Expand or contract the energy field as necessary

Chapter Three: Web Power and Human Spirit Body

Chapter Four: Spirit Helpers

The web of power is also applicable to all of nature's elements. Once you've understand how the spirit is present in everything, you'll eventually learn how to tap into all of nature's resources in ways that you may not have ever imagined. You'll learn how you can use the power of things that are produced by Mother Nature like plants, animals, minerals/ rocks, and other natural beings if you learn on how to communicate with the spirit in all of them.

Chapter Four: Spirit Helpers

For shamans, learning to communicate with such natural objects or creatures only requires one thing, and that is respect. This is the most essential thing when it comes to communication, not just with people but also with objects.

This is probably the reason why in martial arts, masters teach their student to "respect" the weapon that they're using because it will respect them back – one way or another. Any great communicator knows that when it comes to respect, one should carry an openness to connect, and also let go of any judgments. When it comes to natural objects, it is no different as to how these things respond even if you can't see them, what matters is that in one form or another, they'll respond to the respect that you show them.

It's understandable if you feel some sort of skepticism because people are not taught that they can communicate with things like clouds, gems, insects, trees, flowers etc. through one's thoughts and feelings. What you can do is to sort of put yourself into their position, and act as if you're an inanimate object with feelings, and see how people or animals around you respond.

Chapter Four: Spirit Helpers

For shamans, they know that the importance of balance in this world, and the fact that the universe thrive on natural tensions in order to keep the balance. Once the balance is tipped through greed or exploitation, then nature will sort of retaliate. This is why whatever's happening today in the world like global warming, floods, and climate change are all the result of lack of respect for nature thus making the natural world rebels, and creating imbalance.

This chapter will teach you how you can communicate with the spirit helpers like rocks, animals, plants, and other natural elements. Always remember that respect is part of the secret of your success. If you want to be successful in life, and also as a Shaman, you need to cooperate with the environment around you, and learn how to harness real power from the natural forces of this world.

Power of Rocks

The spirit contained inside the rocks has certain vibrations that produce a particular frequency. These types of structures including minerals have various frequency

Chapter Four: Spirit Helpers

types of light and sound. This is very true of gemstones which are made up of concentrated mineral that most people consider very valuable because of its beauty and also practical applications. The different frequencies contained in every mineral or rocks affect the animals, plants and humans around them. Some gemstones produce balance, some are used for healing, while others have various beneficial effects especially for people's health and emotional well – being.

Shamans have mastered on how to communicate with rocks and minerals in the level of its energy, and the influences that these stones give off. They do it by sensing each of the rocks' frequencies and vibrations, and then decide the ones that will have a positive influence and something that brings harmony.

Each gemstones and rocks have specific effects and influences to people and other things because of their different vibrations. We won't discuss each of their influences and effects but the exercises below can help you tune into the spirit of rocks, and make you learn how to speak to them.

Chapter Four: Spirit Helpers

Exercise #1: Rocks, Gemstones, Minerals

Step #1: Choose a certain rock, gemstone or mineral

Step #2: Study the stone and notice every detail in it

Step #3: Close your eyes, and pretend that you're talking to the rock/ stone, and ask about its properties or other information about it like its uses/ purpose etc.

Step #4: Ask the rock/ stone's permission to use these properties in your life. Respect them and ask for their help.

Step #5: Thank the spirit contained within the rock or mineral after speaking to it.

Power of Animals

Just like rocks, every animal has its own power and specialty. What shamans usually do if the problem they're facing or trying to solve has many aspects or is quite complicated is that they consult with different spirit animals. For example, hawks are good at seeing things especially from afar, and the fox is known for its cleverness. Power animals are usually the wild animals, and not your household pets; this is because for shamans, domestic

Chapter Four: Spirit Helpers

animals have already lost their power, and they are better of serving people physically than spiritually unlike wild animals. This is perhaps the reason why wild animals are often used as symbols and emblems in flags, protests, sports teams etc. In some form or another, the power within these wild animals cannot be ignored. It gives us a sense of freedom, camaraderie, and fighting spirit.

So how do shamans find these power animals, and gain mastery? Well for starters, they don't really select one animal, and establish a relationship with it, it's actually the other way around; the animal spirit selects the shaman. Throughout history, the ancients believe that if a shaman or a person survived the attack of a wild animal, it's probably because that animal is the shaman's totem spirit. It just needed to test the man's strength, endurance, and dedication. The shaman must prove to the animal spirit that he/she deserves to handle the power of the spirit animal.

Chapter Four: Spirit Helpers

Exercise #1: Meeting Your Animal Spirit

Step #1: Relax your body and close your eyes

Step #2: Begin your journey of searching your spirit animal in your mind

Step #3: Go to a landscape

Step #4: Have an animal enter that landscape

Step #5: Ask the spirit animal about its qualities, and make sure to listen.

Step #6: Let the image of that animal fade away, and let another power animal come in the landscape

Step #7: Through your search, notice the animal that always comes up in your mind.

Step #8: Give thanks to the animal.

Exercise #2: Honoring Your Spirit Animal

Step #1: Relax your body and close your eyes

Step #2: Greet the spirit animal

Step #3: Assume the animal's posture

Step #4: Become the spirit animal, and also assume that you have its power and qualities

Step #5: Thank the spirit animal, return to your natural posture, and open your eyes.

Power of Plants

In Shamanism, plants are also believed to have spirits, and one should need to know how to communicate with them so that you can both receive mutual benefit. Just like spirit animals, and rocks, plants too, have their own set of frequencies and vibrations. Shamans in every culture know the importance of the plant's properties. Plants are often used for healing and treating ill people. Shamans have discovered the use for each plant that can aid in one's health and well – being. Just like with spirit animals, the more you learn how to communicate with these plants and learn their properties, the more allies you can have, and the more powerful you can become. However, harnessing the spirit from plants is a sort of a specialized field in shamanism. It's up to you if this is something you want to pursue and if you are inclined to take this path.

Chapter Four: Spirit Helpers

When it comes to becoming acquainted with spirits in plants, one need to exercise patience, this is because plants are stationary natural beings, and it experiences life in a very slow pace. It takes time and patience if one wants to get tune in to their vibrations and energetic frequencies. This is again the reason why some people talk or speak to their plants whenever they're planting or watering them so that it will produce great results. As for shamans, what they do is to sit for hours with a plant, and trying to talk to it, listening to it, and sensing its frequencies. The plant eventually tells them their properties.

Exercise #1: Getting to Know Plant Spirits

Step #1: Choose a plant
Step #2: Study the plant, and notice all of its detail
Step #3: Close your eyes, and see the plant and all its detail in your mind, try to include its vibration.
Step #4: Ask about its properties and qualities. Listen to it.
Step #5: Thank the plant and open your eyes
Step #6: Repeat as many times as necessary.

Chapter Four: Spirit Helpers

Chapter Five: Shaping Time and Learning to be in the Present

For shamans, time is very malleable and flexible vessels that can be manipulated with simple know – how. When one learns how to stretch it and also constrict it, it then becomes a powerful tool that's necessary for success. Shamans can bend time by simply going directly to the source. The source is where shamans get access to all sorts of time frames, and because of this, they can gain information or knowledge both from the past and the future. So how do the shamans do this? This is what this chapter is all about.

Chapter Five: Shaping Time & Learning to be in the Present

You'll learn how the shamans "manipulate" time and you'll also learn the advantages of always being present.

Shaping Time

Imagine this for a moment: all present as well as past experiences are being recorded for eternity, say in a giant red record, then imagine that this red record has life and is filled with energy. Visualize that the record also has infinite number of blue records on top of it and below which represents the past and future, and around it are other colors like green, yellow, pink records that represents an alternate circumstance or probably pasts, presents, and futures. Now imagine that shamans are traveling into this, as what they call it "naugal world" or spirit world with animals and other elements as a guide, and emerging at the center of the red record. From this point is where they can gain access to information and knowledge to finding whatever they want or need, it's like a living library or a living record.

It's not just about gaining information but through having immediate access to this world, they can learn to shift the course of events and have an entirely different outcome

Chapter Five: Shaping Time & Learning to be in the Present

or result. However, this doesn't mean that the original circumstance didn't occur; it's just that they can have the ability to input a more desirable outcome through shifting whatever they want into the central point of the record.

Stretching Time

Shamans can manipulate time in various ways. They can stretch it and also make it slow down. There are many incidents from ordinary people who have experienced sort of near death or accident scenarios where they reported that they felt time was slowing down as the moment happens which allowed them to make decisions and also take the necessary action in order to save their lives or prevent further damage. To the shamans, they have the ability to unconsciously do such things because they always carry time warps in them.

Another way that shamans manipulate time is by speeding it up so that a long time goes by very quickly. They can sit still without moving for long periods of time, and be suspended for longer periods. There were lots of shamanic

Chapter Five: Shaping Time & Learning to be in the Present

stories where in order to demonstrate their powers, they asked others to bury them underground for a couple of days and even weeks, when their students dug them up, these shamans emerge very much alive. They truly have the ability to suspend time. Here's an exercise that you can do to enhance your ability in stretching time, you need to use an instrument such as a rattle, percussions, or drum as well as a timer:

Exercise #1: Stretching Time

Step #1: Relax your body, set your alarm for about 4 minutes, and then close your eyes.
Step #2: Begin to drum or rattle (or have someone do it for you)
Step #3: Visualize that you're in a cave, and ask your spirit animal, elemental allies and other spirit guides to help you
Step #4: Increase the tempo of the drumbeat or rattle shake threefold
Step #5: Follow the instructions of your spirit guide
Step #6: Return once you heard the beep of your timer

Chapter Five: Shaping Time & Learning to be in the Present

Step #7: Write down your experience. Chances are you experienced enough to spend longer than 1 hour.

Contracting Time

In order to contract time you need to slide out of your present time frame in ordinary reality or the physical realm. It's pretty much the same when you are asleep for many hours, you're barely aware that time is passing you by. The way to do this is to be so absorbed and involved in your journey (in your mind) that you lose track of time. There's no exercise that can lead an individual to have the ability to contract time. As for shamans, what they do is story telling. They're very good at it, and as you listen, your imagination and being travels to the time frame and location of the story being told. What you can do though is to play tapes of novels or audio books while you're driving or just relaxing. You'll notice how time flies by as you get engaged and absorbed in the story line of the novel you're listening to. It's quite the same with your life, the more exciting it is, the faster time will seem to unfold.

Chapter Five: Shaping Time & Learning to be in the Present
Flying to the Future

Another way that shamans manipulate time is through looking to the future. They take a look at it and then bring back the news of what is going to happen. This is somewhat similar to prophecies and foreseeing which is what shamans are well – known for. They have the ability to travel to the spirit world and enter one of many time tunnels and re – emerge into the "future time." Foreseeing the future has many advantages because you can plan ahead of time, and position yourself in the right place at the right time. But just like in any other magical systems or cultural practices, shamans also know that whatever they see in the future is still not engraved in stone. It's not definite, and it's only based on probabilities. What shamans also know is that whenever they foresee an event, they can find ways to alter it by the present time and avert the situation or perhaps prepare for it.

Chapter Five: Shaping Time & Learning to be in the Present
Exercise #1: Foreseeing the Future

Step #1: Lie down and relax your body

Step #2: Choose a sort of bothersome future circumstance, and then start drumming or rattling.

Step #3: Imagine a cave entrance where you can find your spirit guide. Ask for its help in your journey

Step #5: Journey to see and examine what could be the future.

Step #6: Notice all the details and emotion in a particular event, and see what's wrong about it.

Step #7: Return to your senses and open your eyes. Then reconstruct the event in a 3 dimensional way.

Developing Presence

You might think that shamans, with all their time travel and manipulation, forget where they are. For shamans, they always know where they are in the physical world simultaneously where they are in the spiritual world whenever they're traveling. If shamans don't know where

Chapter Five: Shaping Time & Learning to be in the Present

they are physically, then they can easily resemble a schizophrenic patent or those who have lost touch with the actual world or reality. Shamans are not mentally ill; they are actually masters at what they do through discipline, focus and practice. They learned how to fully control their mind so that they can access the other realms of the universe like the spirit world where they can gain access to things that can help them create a better reality.

If you don't know who you are, then it's probably best that you master first the art of being present in the physical world. Get in touch with your inner self by being in the moment, and being aware of right here, right now. For shamans, the secret to maintaining one's stability is to have an ability to always be present, grounded and balanced. Being present simply means that one should master the present world that one lies in. This means that you need to provide yourself with the basic things you need, make a living, handle challenges, and also care for other people. Shamans don't just live a balanced life in the present but they're also masters of time in other realms. And they also know that they can only be a master of maneuvering

Chapter Five: Shaping Time & Learning to be in the Present

realities if they know how to stay in the present because to them this is where great power lies. They don't worry too much about the past and do wishful thinking for the future because it can remove you from the present moment, what they do is to be conscious of their present moment to manipulate time and create a much desirable reality.

Chapter Five: Shaping Time & Learning to be in the Present

Chapter Six: The Circle of Life

Every shaman knows that in order to create something, something else should first be destroyed. The old form or material is taken apart, and from its energetic source is where something new can arise. Therefore according to Shamanic point of view, all creation is based on some form of destruction. Most of them do not fear something being destroyed because they know that it's part of the cycle of life, and without it life wouldn't exist. Mother Nature shows us the best examples of this cycle of life by constantly destructing something in the form of seasonal changes.

Chapter Six: The Circle of Life

Each season gives way to the next which means that something is destroyed in the process.

Creation and Destruction

You can see the cycle of life in nature. Devastating natural catastrophes like earthquakes, tsunamis, floods, volcanic eruptions, droughts, tornados, and other natural things occur all the time but it is through these that form new life, new landscapes, new lands, new shores, and new possibilities. From a shaman's point of view, destruction is essential because it gives birth to creation, and such transformation is a great power that they've learned on how to use for themselves. If you want to adapt the shamanic way of thinking, then you should be comfortable with the idea of constantly destroying your limiting beliefs so that you can create new perspectives of seeing the world around you. You have to 'die' and leave your own self behind along with your beliefs and other ideas so that you can start learning something new. You need to unlearn what you

Chapter Six: The Circle of Life

have learned. Here's an exercise that can guide you in doing that:

Exercise #1:

Step #1: Relax your body and close your eyes

Step #2: Imagine a cave entrance where you can find your spirit guide whether it's a spirit animal or guardian. Ask for its help in your journey.

Step #3: State your purpose and follow the instructions of your spirit guide

Step #4: Travel to the underworld and find your place to begin

Step #5: Rip your body apart from the skin down to the bones and pile it all up. Burn it down to ash. This is the part where you'll start to unlearn and destroy yourself so that you can create a new you.

Step #6: Thank your guardian and open your eyes. Notice how you feel after the exercise.

Chapter Six: The Circle of Life

Letting Go of Possessions

You have to understand that death and destruction are all integral part of the spirit world or the web of power because it supports new life forms and also creativity. Learning how you can use destruction appropriately and how to get rid of any things that don't contribute to achieving your goals in life is very important. According to shamanistic principles, all of the things you own have some sort of energy or force that you've invested in them which is why anything that you've attached yourself into that drains you and wastes your energy will make you less powerful.

Keep in mind that to a shaman, thoughts and emotions go out and can become attached to anything that they were sent. In order to become more powerful, you have to be less. This is the shamanic way of living. They tend to let go and eliminate all the unnecessary things in their life. Keep in mind that in this context, destroy means to throw away or give away. Getting rid of certain possessions both material and immaterial must be done since these things may no

Chapter Six: The Circle of Life

longer serve you in productive ways. In today's culture, this is known as de – cluttering or being a minimalist. Here are some tips:

- Go through your closet, and toss out the clothes you don't really enjoy wearing anymore.

- Talk to them, and tell thank them for their service, and then mentally let them go.

Letting Go of Beliefs

After letting go of your unnecessary possessions, you have now paved the way to eliminating your limiting, worn out and perhaps obsolete beliefs that once served you but no longer do. This also includes ideas about what you can and can't do and other things that you imagine are not possible. Just like in possessions, your beliefs are also filled with some of your life energy which is why if your mind is filled with opposing beliefs that are no longer appropriate, you tend to become paralyzed and unable to make firm decisions or

Chapter Six: The Circle of Life

even initiate action. This could be an opportunity for you to de – clutter your once long held beliefs and let go of some of it systematically and then discover how closely you have identified with these beliefs because it takes courage and also a broader perspective to be able to let go of these cherished beliefs. You can let go of them without losing your overall integrity as an individual. The following are examples of beliefs that are worthy of letting go or destruction, you can replace it with something new:

Outdated Beliefs	**Replacement**
Only through cheating can one get ahead in life	Honesty can help me get further in life
There's not enough time to accomplish everything	I have all the time that I need to do everything I need to do
There's never enough money for everyone	There's always enough money for all my needs and others
I can do it all by myself, I don't need anyone's help	I can ask for help whenever I need it

Chapter Six: The Circle of Life

Shamanism principles are not real	Shamanism is very real
People prefer not to see my emotions	People are supportive of my feelings
It's hard for women to be successful no matter how intelligent they are	Women can be successful and can also do things that man can do
Men have all the opportunities in life	Women and men can equally get all the opportunities in life
Women make no sense	All people make sense, both women and men
Men are all creeps	Men are loving, respectful, and most are gentlemen.
It's safer to not confront anyone no matter what so that I can't get hurt	It's fine to confront others as long as you know you're in the right
I should take care of everyone else	I should take care of myself best so that I can help others
Everyone's out to get me	Everyone's out to help me
I'm always unlucky	I'm always lucky

Chapter Six: The Circle of Life

I always get taken advantage of	I control my own reality
It's hard for me to get ahead	I can get ahead if I desire it
You have to work very hard just to get ahead	I can get ahead easily
Life isn't fair	Life is just
I need someone to make me happy	I can be happy with myself
I'm the only one who can get the job done	I am one of many who can do a certain job
I'll never change	I'm changing and becoming better everyday
I'm better than everyone else	Everyone else is just as good as I am
Nothing is worth doing	Everything is worth doing
Nobody loves me	Everybody loves me and is happy with my company
I'll never be healthy	I'm always perfectly healthy

Chapter Six: The Circle of Life

Letting Go of Habits

After cleaning up your old and outdated long held beliefs, then perhaps you are ready for a more challenging way of letting go, and that includes getting rid of habits that no longer serve you and may not be at your best interest anymore. Habits include those behavior patterns that you do consciously and subconsciously that keeps you from gaining the greater web of power that's around you. One of the first things you can do to let go of unnecessary habits or your bad habits is by recognizing and being unaware of its patterns. Below are some habitual behaviors that you may want to let go of:

- Traveling the same route to school, work, errands etc.
- Eating the same foods for breakfast, lunch or dinner everyday
- Getting up or going to bed at exactly the same time every day
- Wearing the same clothes everyday

- Using the same figures of speech, metaphors, phrases, or words
- Clearing your throat or nose
- Drinking or smoking a pack every day
- Going to the same restaurant all the time
- Going out with the same people regularly
- Reading the newspaper every day
- Seeing the world from a limited perspective; negatively, cynically, idealistically
- Watching the same programs or watching television too much
- Avoiding being alone
- Avoiding people in general
- Avoiding a certain group of people

Letting Go of Relationships

Letting go of relationships is probably the most difficult thing one can do. According to shamanism, relationships can also drag you down as they support and also reinforce old behavior patterns, beliefs, and habits that

Chapter Six: The Circle of Life

can keep you getting stuck. The hard part is that unlike habits or beliefs that you can transform or turn into something productive once it's destroyed, you can't really change and control how other people respond. What others think and feel about you as a person is essential because people can contribute to your growth, well – being, and also personal satisfaction. Just like possessions and habits, for sure you are carrying a number of relationships that may not already be helpful to you or no longer serve you. According to shamanism, your relationships are very influential when it comes to determining your store of power. It can enhance the power within you through supporting you or contributing in your life, or it can also drain you by undermining your power and abilities.

For shamans, they don't cultivate relationships that won't be of any help to enhancing their personal power. However, this doesn't mean that they're completely avoiding constructive criticism, it just means that they don't continue dealing with relationships that always drains them and attack their ambitions in life because this could be the

Chapter Six: The Circle of Life

very thing that holds a person back in achieving great power. If you know that you're in a toxic relationship with someone, then the more you should let go of it because it won't do you any good in the long run.

Here's how you can start letting go of some of your relationships, follow the tips below:

- Make a list of your relationships – all of it including your family and friends.

- Decide which ones are worth keeping and worth letting go. The relationships that are worthy are almost always shining like a bright light while the one's that deserves to be let go often involved you thinking about it and arguing with yourself.

- List both the positive and negative sides of the relationship, and see if it's balance or if one outweighs another. If you want to keep your relationship with someone who has more negativity, then perhaps you should talk to him/her about these certain negativities. If no amount of communicating will help, then it's better to let it go.

- Have your own set of limitation for each relationship, what goes beyond the line or when it's already too much to handle to the point that it's destroying you inside and in a negative way.

- Once you've made the list, and have weighed the pros and cons, it's time to take your course of action.

Creation

Now that you've seen how important destruction is in life's ongoing flow, and how essential it is to becoming more successful and powerful as an individual from a shamanic point of view, it's now time to learn its opposite which is creation. Once you clear out your life through destruction, you are preparing yourself to open up for more possibilities and creativity.

Chapter Six: The Circle of Life

You'll notice that the web of power ultimately fills your life with pretty much the same things you've gotten rid of, unless you introduce something new, If you want something new, you'll have to give out new desires and instructions to the spirit world, and the spirit realm will notice that you're now ready for something different.

For shamans, they know that they are co – creators with the spirit world, and they use it to gain and manifest power. They practice and use their creativity to help create a more orderly universe and give more meaning to life. According to shamanism, you have to give very specific and clear instructions to the spirit world as to what you want to achieve this is because you'll receive exactly what you ask for.

For instance, let's say you wanted to have a new car because the car that you're currently driving always breaks down. You then say, "I wish I have a different car." Chances are that you'll get a different car but with the same problems. This is because you have given no specific instructions for whatever you wanted to have. You just indicated that you want change but not what kind of change

Chapter Six: The Circle of Life

that will be, which is why you get a different one but the problem of breaking down is still there for some reason. You see, you have to be specific as to what kind of car you want to drive, the specs, the features, and even the price range. Most times people aren't specific and realistic with what they ask for, and often time's people get what they thought they wanted at the moment, only to find out later on that it's not really the thing or person they truly desire. What you get depends on what you believe you think you deserve, and what you believe you think is possible, which is why it's important to let go of limiting beliefs so that you can dream bigger and be limitless.

Creation is one of the most mysterious, magical, and beautiful ability that human beings possessed. We're the only living thing that's gifted with such ability. It all starts with your imagination. The clearer the picture and more specific whatever you want to achieve, the more likely this dream of yours will actualize in the real world. Here's a very simple exercise to illustrate the creation process:

Chapter Six: The Circle of Life

Exercise #1:

Step #1: Relax your body and close your eyes

Step #2: Create a projection screen in your mind

Step #3: Create a flower or trees on the screen

Step #4: Transform its size and color it as much as you'd like

Step #5: See the it bloom, bud, grow, and/or bear fruits

Step #6: Re – create the flower or tree and give it to a loved one. Return.

Chapter Seven: The Worlds of Shamanic Journey

The traditional view of the Shamanic journey is that there are 3 different worlds or three different destinations that a person can travel through while doing the journey. The three worlds are the following includes the Lower World, the Upper World, and the Middle World. They are quite different from each other and are often used for different purposes in the journey. This is what you're going to learn in this chapter

Chapter Seven: The Worlds of Shamanic Journey
The Lower World

This is essentially the world that is down, ground level or in the earth. It is often entered into by going through a hole in the ground or some kind of entry into the earth such as a crack, snake hole, a spring, the space between the bottom of a tree and the ground. There are various ways of entering into the lower world but traditionally it will be a hole in the ground, and then the individual or the shamans will experience something like a tube or some sort of passage way that is the transition between the ordinary reality and the separate reality of the lower world. Eventually at the end of this channel or passage way, the person will encounter some kind of a vista.

The vista is not necessarily a cavern in the earth, although it might often be. However, it's quite different from others because it is very organic, there's a kind of earthy vibes to the lower world journey. It is in this world that shamans encounter animal spirits. It has a lot of connection in the earth, and a lot of communication with the spirit through power animals, and it's also a good place for

Chapter Seven: The Worlds of Shamanic Journey

healing. The lower world is a great place to explore because it's very nurturing, and it has the capability of supporting a shaman or an individual through the journey process as one learns more about it. Usually, beginners are introduced to the lower world to begin their practice of shamanism.

The Upper World

This is the polar opposite of the lower world. You can think of it as being the place that is up and the way to go to the upper world is through climbing a ladder, a rope or going over the rainbow or riding a tornado – anything that'll take a person up. In the modern day context, it can be an elevator where you push the up button or trekking up the mountains. Anyway that makes sense to you of being where you are in the journey to the upper world experience. This journey is where shamans encounter a barrier; one may press up against a cloud or something like that, that doesn't seem to want to move.

Usually this is seen as something like the guardian. As you explore the upper world, and you potentially

Chapter Seven: The Worlds of Shamanic Journey

encounter this barrier, you may or may not be able to get through it – and most of the time, the reason for that is that you may not be ready yet, or maybe something's coming, or there's something you need to know or do before you're able to bypass this guardian. However, when you get into this upper world journey experience, the experience is quite ethereal and very different from the organic lower world. The beings you encountered may be more angelic, or it could be just energy, symbol or color. Sacred geometry is one way that shamans encounter beings in the upper world.

The upper world is where shamans go if they want to look at the larger perspective or see the bigger picture. "What is your life about?" is the kind of question one might pose when going to the upper world. Sometimes this is also where you can meet your original mother and father, or the so – called spirit parents even before you even came to this planet or this life. They may be the ones who know why you're here in this lifetime, which is why having a conversation with these individuals could be fascinating. This is the nature of the upper world journey; sometimes the lower world journey is compared to the story of Alice in

Chapter Seven: The Worlds of Shamanic Journey

Wonderland, while the upper world is compared to the story of the Wizard of Oz where the main character rides the tornado and landed on the other world full of different kinds of beings.

The Middle World

The middle world is where we are right now. It is the world of our everyday lives, and it includes everything that we know about our reality system. In the middle world journey, you can virtually journey anywhere and any when because the middle world also includes concepts of time. In the middle world experience, you can journey into your past, and the potential futures which are both legitimate destinations in this world. You can communicate with people but when you're communicating with them in the middle world journey, you're not necessarily talking to them as though you were sitting across the room and speaking to them, you're usually communicating with their energy and spirit.

Chapter Seven: The Worlds of Shamanic Journey

You can think of it as a world that has shifted energetically, just a little bit off of the physical reality making you communicate with anything or anyone like a person, your dog, a tree, or someone on the other side of the planet or even travel outside the earth because it's all part of this known reality. The middle world is a place where you can get some real work done in terms of energetic connections with people or things and also speak to the relationship between things.

These are the three different worlds according to Shamanism. As you have learned, each one of them is fundamentally different and unique. Each one of them also has their own kind of power. This is why shamans can choose the best destination or journey they want that fits a certain world. You can intend to go on the lower world for healing, or the upper world to gain perspective, or the middle world so that you can communicate with what's here and now.

Chapter Eight: Shamanic Healing

Shamanic healing is an essential application in shamanic practices that incorporates everything the practitioner knows to that point and can build upon in terms of their own experience and understanding of how spirit works. The important thing about shamanic healing is that, it's not really about the practitioner doing the work, in fact its job is to get out of the way, to set aside one's own mind or ambition, and one's own importance and let the spirit blow

Chapter Eight: The Astral Projection

through since the healing is done by spirit not by the practitioner.

Hollow Bone Concept

There's a concept called the "hollow bone." The Shaman healer's job is to be as hollow as a bone as they can which involves clearing themselves out so that they're available for the spirit to move through the shaman and do its work without them getting involved in the process. In simple terms, the spirit uses the body of the shaman healer to get the job done. Therefore, healing can't entirely be attached to the practitioner.

We're all energy beings. All people are here in physical form but fundamentally we are energy. Therefore, the work that is done in shamanic healing is energy working with energy; or spirit working with spirit. Sometimes, the healing is nothing more than helping a person's energy to flow more purely and clearly, and to also be more in balanced. From a shamanic perspective, being ill or handling

Chapter Eight: The Astral Projection

an illness is about being out of balance. Fundamentally we are all whole or well all the time, the problem is that we tend to get in the way of our own physicality. People tend to attached fears or other things that interrupts the flow. What a shaman healer does is to find those places that are out of balance, and return them to balance either physically, mentally, emotionally or spiritually in order to get them back to harmony.

The shaman almost always finds a way to identify where the individual is out of balance, and return that into balance. A lot of healing that's done is done in the energetic body, often in spirit or the mental/ emotional/ physical bodies but it's always done in the next level. We have the physical body, we have the mental and emotional body which is larger, and we also have the spirit or soul that's larger than that. The approach of healing should be from the outside in. One should take care of the problem of the mental/ emotional body before it becomes solid that it manifests in the physical body. From a shamanic perspective, you should not just work on the illness of the physical body but also the energy body so that the imprint is healed or removed and will not re - assert itself.

Soul Retrieval

Another important thing when it comes to shamanic healing is that sometimes the problem that shows up isn't coming from the present moment rather an incident from the past or from your childhood, or an accident, or any traumatic experiences. There are a lot of different instances where people can be injured in their soul. There's what shamans call "soul retrieval." This is where they go through a journey into the personal history to find the soul part which is needed by the person in this point of time. They'll literally go back to the person's history until they encounter that soul part with the intention of taking it and bringing it back, and making it available once again for the individual. It can be envisioned as another aspect of oneself.

There's a difference between the soul retrieval process and counseling because what a lot of counselors are afraid of

Chapter Eight: The Astral Projection

is to re – traumatize an individual, and so they can get to the point where there's a dip and they move on past it, and don't necessarily get to the bottom which is what's needed, and must gain access to the soul part that was once lost.

Reliving the Moment

There's an aspect of soul retrieval that you can do for yourself. Essentially what that involves is you being able to go back to that place, to that incident, and relive that incident in your life fully; what it looks like, what it sounded like, who said what, how it smelled, how it felt, how solid it was etc.

Do your very best to completely and totally relive that moment or event. And having done that, you can change the end, you can make things turn out differently through reclaiming the energy of that experience since you've lost some form of energy there so that you bring that back. You have to hold the image in your mind, and bring it forward and use it to the parts of the body that needed that energy.

Chapter Eight: The Astral Projection

On the other hand, there could be some situations that people encounter that's too personal and you might not get enough objectivity where you can be able to go into it and also avoid getting trapped by it again. At that point, this is where a shaman healer/ practitioner can help you to go through that or go through the journey for you. On this day and age, people accept responsibility in their lives much more than in the past, and so it makes sense then to empower ourselves to this kind of deep healing and at the same time, it's very important that you have someone there to guide you or help you work your way through it.

Another aspect that makes it difficult to heal people is when they can't remember significant traumas. There are a lot of people who don't remember much of anything which is why it's important that a shaman healer can go back to the personal history to retrieve information that one can't remember.

Chapter Nine: Ritual and Ceremonies of Shamanism

Rituals and ceremonies are part of ancient shamanism, and its forms are practiced in different cultures and countries. According to shamans, rituals or ceremonies are the channel that connects the spirit world with our ordinary world or physical reality. The shamans uses ordinary elements found in nature like crystals, herbs, fires, circles, sage, and other natural phenomena. During such rituals and ceremonies, all of the senses are incorporated to

Chapter Nine: Ritual and Ceremonies of Shamanism

ensure that one will experience the web of power fully, and also use one's power to shift, transform and also create. In this chapter, you'll learn the basic Shamanic rituals.

Rituals and Ceremonies

Whenever shamans want to manifest their power, they do it through a ritual. This is because by doing this, they are being reminded of the important source of power of the spirit realm, and they're also reminded of the shamanic principles and basics. The ritual is also a way for them to remember to ask for what they truly desire or seek. It functions as a focus where they can ask for assistance via spiritual guardians, connect fully with the web of power, and also imagine their goals as well as surrender and perhaps destroy old beliefs/ let go of some things to create new outcomes.

Chapter Nine: Ritual and Ceremonies of Shamanism

Characteristic of Rituals and Ceremonies

As mentioned earlier, during rituals, shamans use simple natural elements like fire, crystals, stones etc. that is based on ancient shamanic practices. These natural elements are what are still being used today in the modern time. When it comes to rituals, it's usually similar to opening ceremonies such as sports, graduations, international events, festivities, and other religious gatherings. Rituals and ceremonies are characterized by the following; this is what you may encounter once you attend a shamanic practice:

- Invoking the power of sound through drumming, chanting, singing, used of musical instruments

- Invoking the power of movement through postures, hand and body movements, gestures

- Invoking the power of smell through fire, burning incense, crystals, salt etc.

- Invoking the power of location by performing it in what they call sacred spots

Chapter Nine: Ritual and Ceremonies of Shamanism

- Invoking the power of guardians through inviting the presence and participation of power animals or spirit animals as well as other elemental allies

- Invoking the power of the people around them by requesting prayers or joint focus of attention.

Rituals and ceremonies also have the following characteristics:

- It is usually done on significant dates and times or natural phenomena like equinox, new moon, full moon, all soul's day, arrival of monsoons, mid – summer etc.

- It can be performed at significant rites like birthday, marriage, death, puberty, or when one is initiated into positions of authority or power.

Chapter Nine: Ritual and Ceremonies of Shamanism

- It can be performed during the opening and closing of important meetings when a council comes to an agreements like towards certain laws or regulations.

- It is performed to signal a transfer to a different world, state of consciousness or to begin a mental journey.

- It is usually performed to commemorate important events or celebrate events like the birth/ death of a renowned leader, Independence Day, victory from oppression etc.

- It's usually performed when one is physically or emotionally ill or during a profound event.

Most modern – day shamans will suggest that one should use rattles which is an ancient shamanic tool. It is quite a strange thing for adults since rattles are commonly used for babies but it's something that many shamans throughout the ages and throughout the world used when performing rituals and ceremonies as it has some powerful significance during the invoking practices.

Rattles are usually made from dried gourds with pebbles or small beans placed inside to create a rattling sound effect. Usually the contents are passed on from one shaman to another, or the materials are found in sacred sites or power spots. The gourds are attached to a stick and are decorated with various designs. These are often made to resemble animals or elementals from the spirit realm because for shamans, the sound that it creates is a way to open the door of the spirit world. It is also a helpful tool to call the power animals and elemental allies or spirit guardians.

The drum is thought to carry the shamans to and from the spirit realm, but the rattle bring the spirit realm and all the spiritual beings closer to our physical world or ordinary reality. The sound produced by a rattle also invokes an altered state due to its high – pitched frequency. It is highly recommended that you use rattles along with other tools like drums because all of these are effective materials for setting up the ritual and opening the ceremony.

Chapter Nine: Ritual and Ceremonies of Shamanism

Symbolic Death Rites

The initial tasks of shamans in traditional communities are to be healers and also teachers. They then observed that the problem with illnesses is that it can definitely be fatal, so they set a goal to cure and heal death, but the question is how do we escape from death itself? Before you learn that, you have to first learn some important concepts on how shamans approached it.

According to shamanism, the luminous body is released from the physical body at the moment of death, and then it will follow the journey into the spiritual world or the invisible realm of formlessness. The moment that death occurs upon an individual, the electrical activity of the brain and body ceases. This electrical activity in effect is to hold the luminous body in the physical body.

There are two things that hold a soul down to its physical form according to shamanism; the first one is the electromagnetic field that's cause by electricity or electrons travelling along the long nerves of the body. When the

Chapter Nine: Ritual and Ceremonies of Shamanism

activity ceases or when a person dies, the electromagnetic field drops to zero, and the luminous body is set free. The second one is known as the Shakras (which is something that you always heard in Hinduism or other religious practices/systems). The Shakras in the body are the "screw points" where the luminous body is actually attached or screwed to the physical body. During the process of healing, the shaman clears accumulated debris or baggage inside it, that has built up in the shakras, so that at the moment of death they can be set free in their journey back home without anything holding them back.

Death rites are being done in many shamanic practices around the world. This is designed to assist a loved one, to journey consciously back home into the world of spirit. There are three steps to the death rites; the first one is recapitulation, the next is giving permission to die, and the last is the technical part of disengaging the luminous energy field which is done by spinning the shakras in a counter – clockwise direction in a giant spiral beginning with the heart shakra, down to the solar plexus, then back up on the throat shakra, then the belly shakra, then the third eye in the

Chapter Nine: Ritual and Ceremonies of Shamanism

middle of the forehead, next is the shakra at the base of the spine, and then up to the crown of 7 shakras which is at the top of the head. This is what they call the unwinding of the great spiral.

According to the shamans, when we die, all of the information in the shakras sort of uploads itself from each one of the 7 shakras into the 8th shakra; the 8th shakra is basically a radiant sun that we have high above our heads that you may have seen from images depicted from Jesus Christ or Buddha. It's a bright radian sun above our heads. It is the luminous body that we occupy in between incarnations. The job of the 8th shakra, resembling a halo that you also see among saints, is to create physical bodies. So when we are reborn, the information from the 8th shakra which is the previous information from our 7 shakras in our former lifetime sort of downloads into a new body, and installs itself into each 7 shakras of the new child that's now in the womb. It transmits the information about the we're going to live, the karma we're going to have, the people we're going to meet and the lessons we need to learn, the

Chapter Nine: Ritual and Ceremonies of Shamanism

way we're going to love and live, and also the way we're going to die.

The task of the shaman is to clear the shakras or the imprint of each of the 7 shakras so we're not born again into a toxic family, or are not born again in a body that's going to be guided by karma, suffering or disease. During our lifetime, one must clear its own shakras. For shamans, when a person is able to clear all of its shakras, one tends to acquire the jaguar body which is the body of the rainbow jaguar that's also identical with what the Tibetans talk about. Your shakras are now shining with the colors of the rainbow, and aren't affected by trauma or all the challenges that you suffered in your lifetime. Your shakra will glow into your original and pure nature, and once you've acquired this rainbow body, you'll leap like the jaguar between this lifetime and infinity. At this moment, you'll also be able to break free from the great cycle of birth and death. You can become totally enlightened into the spirit world, and become free of the suffering of reincarnation and rebirth that all of us may be subject to.

Chapter Nine: Ritual and Ceremonies of Shamanism

Shamanic Maps to the Journey beyond Death

So how do you clear these stale energies from each of your shakras so that you can acquire the rainbow body? This section will focus on teaching you on how to map what happens when you cross that threshold, what happens after the moment of death.

The shamans from the Americas and the shamans of Tibet were the great cartographers of the soul. They had mapped out the journey to infinity, and they have used the technique known as deep meditation to displace consciousness outside the body or the realms beyond the gateway of death. There had been ancient maps that had been drafted by shamans in different part of the world, across different cultures; these maps to the domains beyond death that we will all experience at the very critical time in our lives. You must prepare for it because this is perhaps the most extraordinary journey that you'll ever undertake.

Chapter Nine: Ritual and Ceremonies of Shamanism

What usually happens when one dies is very similar when you're having a lucid dream. This is where your consciousness extends to a hundred fold and you become aware of everything around you. If in that moment you can realize your oneness in creation that you are part of and at the same time a great witness to creation unfolding at that instant, then you can become enlightened, and attain great liberation.

For the shamans, one of the most important parts of their training is how they'll die consciously, and how they'll transmit their consciousness into infinity at the moment of death. Part of the shaman's training is how to get out of this life alive.

The process is quite simple. It begins by healing oneself, through cleaning toxic debris inside each of our shakras that defined our identity. Once you've learned how to do this then you can break out from the hand of karma, you can then break away from the grip of fate, and step to your calling or destiny so you can dedicate yourself into your purpose here in this lifetime.

Chapter Ten: Bringing Shamanism to Life

Shamanism is a practical practice, and the main reason why one should do shamanic practices is to make a difference in their own lives or the lives of others. The most important thing in doing this art or using this system is to find ways on how you can use and integrate the concepts and principles of shamanism into your life. How you bring the practices, belief systems, understandings out of the journey and into your everyday existence, your everyday behaviors and your relationships with others.

Chapter Ten: Bringing Shamanism to Life

That is really the core of shamanism, and what shamanic practice is all about.

How to Bring Shamanism to Life

How do you bring the practice of working with animal spirits, for instance, in your everyday life? How do you bring the context of "everything is alive" into your everyday life? These are two of the biggest parts of Shamanic practices.

Working with animal spirits in your everyday life is a powerful way of changing your life from being sort of a mundane and ordinary kind of existence to being a magical existence that incorporates the flow of spirit all the time. One practice that's quite effective that some shamans use is called "morning messenger." This is a very simple method, and also takes very little time to do but it's something that one needs to practice daily or for quite some time in order to get it.

Chapter Ten: Bringing Shamanism to Life

Morning Messenger

Most of the time when people wakes up they have their own rituals that they do like brushing their teeth, getting coffee or getting dressed, and usually after that wakening ritual is done, they prepare themselves for work, then they go out, jump in their car, and drove off to work. I'm sure most of you do this every day, and it becomes a routine, and after a while it becomes part of their habit, it's automatic, and you don't have to think about it anymore. It becomes part of your day to get by in order to go on to your job.

Most shamans will suggest that you break that habit or that routine, and you can do it plainly simply and interestingly by taking just 5 minutes like whenever you leave your house or before you get into your car, why not go seat on your front porch, and just observe what's going on around you.

You can start looking for things that capture your attention such as an animal or a plant, a cloud etc. Look for something interesting if you can and notice what that is. Let's say for example you saw a squirrel; what is that

Chapter Ten: Bringing Shamanism to Life

squirrel doing? What are squirrels? Why are they here? You can then take that symbol to your day and keep that in mind from time to time, like what's that squirrel trying to say to me? What is it trying to tell me on how I should live my day today? You'll soon notice that whatever you're doing has a particular pattern to it, and you may realize that if you were in tune with that pattern everything will flow really well.

This could be some of your realizations depending on the thing or being that captured your attention in a particular day. This simple exercise can bring more spirit into your, what seem to be an ordinary day, that it wouldn't be if you've just gone on to your usual routine. This is one way that you can stop being so normal and following your routine, and allow the spirit to communicate to you about what's going on through your day.

Inviting Your Power Animals

This is another idea that you can be quite fun. You can invite your power animals to join you in your everyday life; on your journey you can go visit them in their home,

Chapter Ten: Bringing Shamanism to Life

why not invite them to visit them into yours? This is a way of incorporating your animal spirit into your everyday existence. You can invite a power animal at work, and show them what you do for a living or let them wander around and visit your co – workers, then perhaps later have a conversation about that with your power animal.

These are just some of the ways on how you can communicate and urge spirit to be part of your life. Of course, it will take a little bit of imagination and it will take a willingness to play but it can be very rewarding. These are just 2 simple ways that you can begin to open the door to allow spirits and move through you.

What we're really looking for, if you think about it and wondering how you to incorporate spirits into your everyday life, how you can incorporate shamanism into your everyday life, is to recognize how spiritual everything really is already, and that there's a great aspect about shamanism which has to do with recognizing that everything is alive, and everything can be spoken to, and that everything can be honored and respected.

Chapter Ten: Bringing Shamanism to Life

You can express your gratitude to your things even the ones you think are just machines like your phone or computer, or your car. This is a great way to bring shamanism into your life.

Photo Credits

Page 1 Photo by user Activedia via Pixabay.com, https://pixabay.com/en/shaman-spiritual-spirit-tribal-2897334/

Page 6 Photo by user Kalhh via Pixabay.com, https://pixabay.com/en/dream-catcher-a-cultural-object-2705053/

Page 16 Photo by user Allinoch via Pixabay.com, https://pixabay.com/en/fire-witch-girl-jumping-flies-2914766/

Page 29 Photo by Allinoch user via Pixabay.com, https://pixabay.com/en/fire-autumn-shaman-girl-twilight-2837835/

Page 36 Photo by user Staceylemire via Pixabay.com, https://pixabay.com/en/paco-peru-peruvian-landscape-1694024/

Page 44 Photo by user Devanath via Pixabay.com, https://pixabay.com/en/tribal-shaman-rave-drum-drumstick-1215112/

Page 52 Photo by user 8 moments via Pixabay.com,

https://pixabay.com/en/shamanism-spirituality-shaman-2100949/

Page 65 Photo by user Activedia via Pixabay.com, https://pixabay.com/en/fractal-abstract-artistic-764921/

Page 71 Photo by user Antranias via Pixabay.com, https://pixabay.com/en/nature-ritual-rituals-indians-258140/

Page 77 Photo by user Bill Damon via Pixabay.com, https://www.flickr.com/photos/billdamon/7301904932/

Page 82 Photo by user mdhondt via Pixabay.com, https://pixabay.com/en/friends-shaman-happy-beard-1861499/

References

Classic Shamanism and Core Shamanism: Basic Differences – Northern Shamanism.org

http://www.northernshamanism.org/classic-core-shamanism.html

Finding Balance – Wicca.com

https://wicca.com/celtic/wyldkat/balance.htm

Getting Back to the Basics - Shamanism.com

https://www.shamanism.com/journal/getting-back-to-the-basics

Introduction to Shamanic Practices – Shaman's Cave

https://www.shamanscave.com/practices/introduction-to-shamanic-practices

Origins of Shamanism – Gaia.com

https://www.gaia.com/lp/content/how-much-do-you-know-about-shamanism/

Power Animals and Spirit Guides – Personal Tao

https://personaltao.com/soul-spirit/power-animal-retrieval/

Power Animals:
Spirit Helpers in Animal Form - Shamanism-101.com

http://www.shamanism-101.com/Power_Animals.html

Shamanism – Wikipedia.org

https://en.wikipedia.org/wiki/Shamanism

Shamanism Basics – BeliefNet.com

http://www.beliefnet.com/faiths/pagan-and-earth-based/2003/12/shamanism-basics.aspx

Shamanic Healing in the Northern Tradition - Northern Shamanism.org

http://www.northernshamanism.org/shamanic-healing.html

Shamanic Ritual and Practice Introduction and Overview - Shamanism-101.com

http://www.shamanism-101.com/Shamanism_Practice_Ritual.html

Shamanic Ritual: The Heart of Transformation - Gaia.com

https://www.gaia.com/article/shamanic-ritual

Step Into The World Of Shamanism – The Culture Trip

https://theculturetrip.com/europe/france/paris/articles/step-into-the-world-of-shamanism/

Three Worlds Non Ordinary Reality – Shamanic Journey.com

http://www.shamanicjourney.com/three-worlds-nonordinary-reality

What is a Power Animal? - Earthmagic.net

http://www.earthmagic.net/shamanic-journey/what-is-a-power-animal/

Web of Power – Wicca.com

https://wicca.com/celtic/wyldkat/pwrspirit.htm

The 7 Keys to Accessing Shamanic Consciousness: An In-Depth Guide to Understanding and Practicing Shamanism – Conscious Lifestyle Magazine

https://www.consciouslifestylemag.com/shamanism-healing-practices-keys/

The Three Worlds of Shamanism – Organic - Unity.com

http://www.organic-unity.com/top-menu/the-three-worlds-of-shamanism/

Feeding Baby
Cynthia Cherry
978-1941070000

Axolotl
Lolly Brown
978-0989658430

Dysautonomia, POTS Syndrome
Frederick Earlstein
978-0989658485

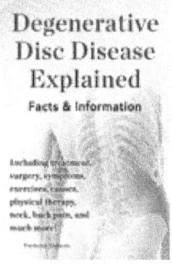

Degenerative Disc Disease Explained
Frederick Earlstein
978-0989658485

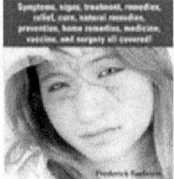

Sinusitis, Hay Fever,
Allergic Rhinitis Explained
Frederick Earlstein
978-1941070024

Wicca
Riley Star
978-1941070130

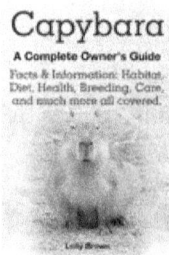

Zombie Apocalypse
Rex Cutty
978-1941070154

Capybara
Lolly Brown
978-1941070062

Eels As Pets
Lolly Brown
978-1941070167

Scabies and Lice Explained
Frederick Earlstein
978-1941070017

Saltwater Fish As Pets
Lolly Brown
978-0989658461

Torticollis Explained
Frederick Earlstein
978-1941070055

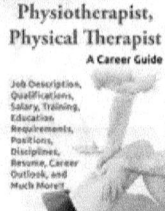

Kennel Cough
Lolly Brown
978-0989658409

Physiotherapist, Physical Therapist
Christopher Wright
978-0989658492

Rats, Mice, and Dormice As Pets
Lolly Brown
978-1941070079

Wallaby and Wallaroo Care
Lolly Brown
978-1941070031

Bodybuilding Supplements
Explained
Jon Shelton
978-1941070239

Demonology
Riley Star
978-19401070314

Pigeon Racing
Lolly Brown
978-1941070307

Dwarf Hamster
Lolly Brown
978-1941070390

Cryptozoology
Rex Cutty
978-1941070406

Eye Strain
Frederick Earlstein
978-1941070369

Inez The Miniature Elephant
Asher Ray
978-1941070353

Vampire Apocalypse
Rex Cutty
978-1941070321

www.ingramcontent.com/pod-product-compliance
Lightning Source LLC
LaVergne TN
LVHW051645080426
835511LV00016B/2511